Introduc

Following on from *"At The Going Down of the Sun"*, *"Lest We Forget"* is my second collection of World Wars One and Two themed poems. Many of the poems are again inspired by some of my 485 relatives who died during the two wars. Some of the poems have been written especially to commemorate notable anniversaries taking place over the last few years, whilst others focus on more hard-hitting topics of war such as the holocaust, conscientious objectors, those who were shot at dawn and shell shock to name but a few. Whilst the poems have been written predominantly with World Wars One and Two in mind, some of them are equally relevant to other conflicts since then and to present day conflicts.

Poetry is a unique way of telling a story and each poem in this book has its own story, which in many cases is based on true accounts and real people.

I hope you find the poems moving and thought provoking. They are accompanied by photos taken from visits to war graves, memorials and museums around the UK and abroad.

Lest We Forget

Lest We Forget

Becky Bishop

A collection of war poems

Other books by Becky Bishop

Poetry

At The Going Down of the Sun

Seasons of Change

Sequins and Sparkles (Strictly Come Dancing 2019)

WW2

With all my love, Melvin.

Dedication

In loving memory of Gunner William George Foxworthy (1880 - 1918)

"no longer a forgotten casualty"

Lest We Forget

Contents

No longer a forgotten casualty	15
Special Operations Executive	17
Black Sheep Soldier	20
D-Day 75	23
Returning from war	26
The Armistice	29
To my dear son	33
Persecuted	35
After Effects of War	41
The Poppy	43
Conscripted	47
On the beaches of Dunkirk	51
Christmas Truce	55
In Mourning	60
Remembrance Day	61
The Evacuee	65
Prisoner of War	69
White Feather	71
Conscientious Objector	76
Blood red tears	79
VE Day 75	81
When you see a poppy think of me	85
Will you remember me?	89
Dunkirk 80	92
My young lad	94
Battle of Britain 80	97
Shot at Dawn	100

"When you go home
Tell them of us and say,
For your tomorrow
We gave our today"

William's grave in St Clements churchyard, Dartmouth. Photo courtesy of Ted Guthrie

No longer a forgotten casualty

In memory of Gunner William George Foxworthy

When war broke out, I joined up to fight,
Together with my brother, we thought we were doing what was right.

The following year I was sent to France and into the trenches,
Amongst all the bloodshed, mud and the stench.

It was out here some months later, that I got taken ill,
I was sent to hospital but it wasn't something, that could be cured with pills.

I was discharged from the army and suffered with tuberculosis for two years,
I died two months after my brother was killed, causing my family many tears.

In a churchyard near my home, I was buried with my parents in a grave,
Unlike my brother, I wasn't considered an official casualty of war or one of the brave.

For almost one hundred years, things stayed the same,
Until 2017 when a relative, made the CWGC aware of my name.

My case was under review for two years, by now one hundred and one years since I'd died,
Then the day came I was declared an official casualty and could finally be remembered with pride.

Now I'm waiting for a war grave, my name will be there for all to see,
One hundred and two years after my death, people will finally be able to remember me.

Just like my brother, I finally get the recognition and honour I deserve at last,
No longer a forgotten casualty, of a war long past.

Special Operations Executive

I've been asked to undertake a new mission,
that's happening in France,
There's a likelihood I could be captured and
killed but I'm willing to take a chance.

I'm dropped from a plane into France, in the
dead of night,
I have to be alert and hide my parachute
quickly out of sight.

For I don't know who may be watching, there
may be German patrols around,
I have to stay quiet and keep close to the
ground.

Each mission has its risks but there are many
operatives like me who are doing the same,
We're not known by our real names, instead
we're given code names.

Eventually someone collects me and takes me
to where I'll stay,
I have a cover story, I have a role to play.

I must be very careful who I speak to, you
never know who is a foe,
I have to transmit messages, back to Britain
they'll go.

Each time I hear footsteps on the stairs, I think it's the Germans and I tremble on the spot,
For if the Germans find me here, the family protecting me will be shot.

There are many operatives like myself, we have a plan for if the time comes,
We have a pill to swallow, rather than tell our secrets to the Hun.

So many of my colleagues have been captured, tortured and haven't survived,
I must stay one step ahead, I want to stay alive.

Black Sheep Soldier

In memory of Private Roland William Austin

Life was going well, I had two young kids and a lovely wife,

And then the war came, bringing trouble and strife.

Like so many men, I joined up to fight,

I thought I was doing my duty, doing what was right.

I stood proudly in my uniform, the day I went away,

Off to the battlefields, little did I know the price I'd have to pay.

I was killed at Passchendaele, for me no one cried any tears,

Cast as the black sheep of the family, my name was never mentioned for years.

And why you might wonder, was I cast in this way,
For just doing what other men did, when war came that day.

Like me, all the other men, had to leave their families behind,
But my family thought I was wrong, when my death left them in a bind.

But one day I'll be remembered and seen in a new light,
Someone will be proud of me, for doing my duty and what I thought was right.

D-Day 75

75 years it's been, since troops landed on the beach,
Taking part in an invasion, hoping victory was within reach.

For months they were preparing, for the invasion that was to come,
In what was hoped would be, the start of the downfall of the Hun.

Originally planned for 5th June but bad weather held them back,
Instead the following day, allied forces launched their attack.

Codenamed operation Overlord but better
known as D-Day,
Landing on the assault beaches, the attack was
under way.

The Americans took Utah and Omaha
beaches, the British took Sword and Gold,
The Canadians took Juno, our troops were
brave and bold.

By the end of August, they'd liberated
northern France,
And in the battle against the Germans, this
was their biggest chance.

The Normandy invasion was a success but
victory came at a price,
For many taking part, they paid with their
life.

The boot prints they left in the sand, the sea
long ago washed them away,
If only we could thank them, for the part they
played that day.

All these years later on the anniversary, we
honour those who fought and died,
They won't ever be forgotten, we'll remember
them with pride.

Returning from War

My husband's come home but he doesn't seem the same,

A shadow of his former self, he can barely remember my name.

His eyes once bright blue, are now dull and haunted with worry,

His voice is a whisper, he keeps saying sorry.

He needs feeding up, he's so weak and gaunt,

He cries out in his sleep, nightmares of war they haunt.

He sits quietly in his chair, not a word is spoken,

He stares into space, his mind seems so broken.

Where's the man I married, he is no more,

Left on the battlefield, damaged by war.

As time goes by, he slowly starts to come back,
Still not quite the same but still my beloved Jack.

The Armistice

11am on the Eleventh of November,
A day like no other, one I'll always remember.

At the time we were in the trenches, lying in wait for the Hun,
Preparing to do battle, getting ready to fire our guns.

Four years we've been fighting, we've lost many a friend,
And now we've been told, the war's finally at an end.

We might have won but victory came at a cost,
For nothing can replace, all the lives that were lost.

They lie side by side in cemeteries, at least they're not alone,
And for those of us who survived, we can make the journey home.

Away from the battlefields, the dirt and the dust,

Once we're back home, it takes a while to adjust.

Life has changed, whilst I've been gone,

Buildings have disappeared and people have moved on.

There's family and friends, I haven't seen for a while,

I try to look cheerful and conjure a smile.

But they can't comprehend, the horrors I saw,

They think it all disappeared, once I walked back through the door.

The memories are always there, as the years go by,

I'll never speak of what happened, nor will I cry.

As time moves on, the war becomes a thing of the past,

But the part we played, leaves a legacy that'll last.

Each year on Armistice Day, we wear our poppies with pride,

We lay wreaths at memorials, to commemorate all those who died.

We hold two minutes silence and play the last post,

As we remember the brave and the sacrifice of a generation lost.

Donald Freear (1924 – 2018)

To my dear son

In memory of Donald Freear

To my dear son,

Hope you're well lad, as Mam and I are here,
Oh how we miss you, how we wish you were near.

It seems so long, since your last leave in June,
But the news seems good, hopefully the war will end very soon.

The end can't come soon enough, the war's gone on far too long,
And then you and Ted will be home, back where you belong.

So that's all for now lad, keep smiling and God Bless,
I'll write again soon, good luck and all the best.

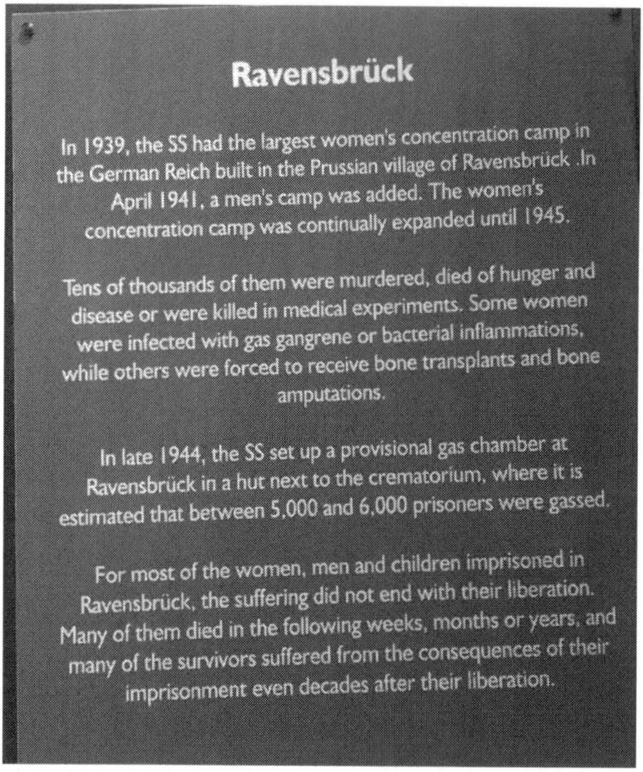

Ravensbrück

In 1939, the SS had the largest women's concentration camp in the German Reich built in the Prussian village of Ravensbrück .In April 1941, a men's camp was added. The women's concentration camp was continually expanded until 1945.

Tens of thousands of them were murdered, died of hunger and disease or were killed in medical experiments. Some women were infected with gas gangrene or bacterial inflammations, while others were forced to receive bone transplants and bone amputations.

In late 1944, the SS set up a provisional gas chamber at Ravensbrück in a hut next to the crematorium, where it is estimated that between 5,000 and 6,000 prisoners were gassed.

For most of the women, men and children imprisoned in Ravensbrück, the suffering did not end with their liberation. Many of them died in the following weeks, months or years, and many of the survivors suffered from the consequences of their imprisonment even decades after their liberation.

Persecuted

The Germans have invaded our country and
the rumours really are true,
That people are being persecuted, just for
being Jews.

We've been told we have to register, we're
spat at and abused in the street,
A curfew is imposed, we must be careful who
we meet.

We don't know who to trust anymore, friends
are turning into foes,
We should have left the country but now it's
too late to go.

Then one day we're rounded up like cattle, loaded onto different trucks to take us away,
Across the trucks our eyes meet, as we try to convey the words we want to say.

On one truck there's me, my two sisters, Aunt and Mother,
On another there's my Father, Uncle, Cousin and brothers.

We huddle together on the trucks, conditions are cold and damp,
The journey is bumpy and in our hearts we know, we're being taken to a concentration camp.

For we've heard the rumours about these camps, we've heard of people being starved, tortured and abused,
We've heard of friends who've died, you have to be strong to see it through.

Once we arrive my Mother and two little
sisters are sent to the left, my Aunt and I are
sent to the right,
The following day we find out, my Mother
and sisters were gassed that very night.

I wonder what's happened to the rest of my
family, I hope they're still alive,
My Aunt and I have to do our best, to make it
out of here and survive.

We're soon put to work, the weeks turn into
months and the months turn into years,
I think of my mother and sisters daily and for
them I cry many tears.

We're beaten for no reason, other women are
raped and abused,
Abortions are performed, it's so degrading
being used.

Disease and illness is rife within camp, we've grown so thin and weak,
We're all just skin and bone, our ribs hurt when we try and speak.

My Aunt succumbs to illness, the next day the camp is liberated,
I'll finally make it out of here but for my aunt it came just a day too late.

I think of all the friends I've made in camp, so many of whom have died,
And the ones like me who survived, have a haunted look in their eyes.

I think we'll never forget, this hell hole that we've been,
Nor forget all the suffering and horrors, during our time in camp we've seen.

Sometime later, I finally make it back to my home,
I hope my father and brothers have survived,
I don't want to be all alone.

Then one day my Uncle and older brother appear at the door, they're the only ones to have survived,
I weep for my father, cousins and younger brother but the three of us are lucky to be alive.

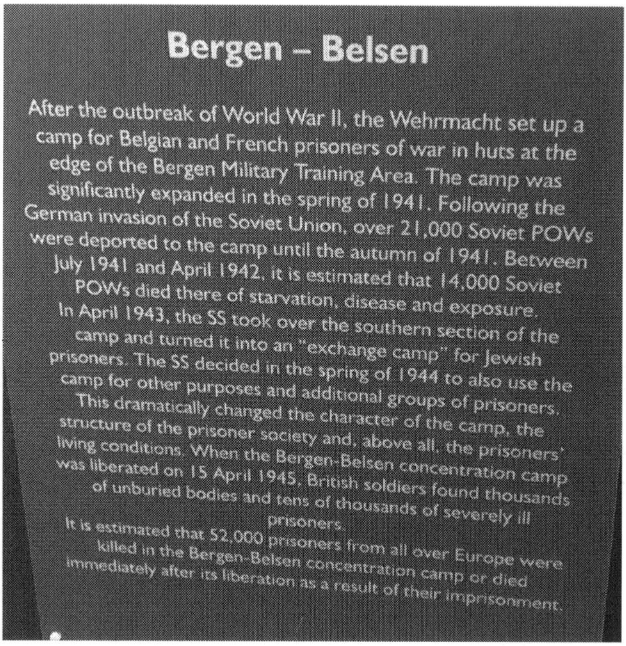

Bergen – Belsen

After the outbreak of World War II, the Wehrmacht set up a camp for Belgian and French prisoners of war in huts at the edge of the Bergen Military Training Area. The camp was significantly expanded in the spring of 1941. Following the German invasion of the Soviet Union, over 21,000 Soviet POWs were deported to the camp until the autumn of 1941. Between July 1941 and April 1942, it is estimated that 14,000 Soviet POWs died there of starvation, disease and exposure.

In April 1943, the SS took over the southern section of the camp and turned it into an "exchange camp" for Jewish prisoners. The SS decided in the spring of 1944 to also use the camp for other purposes and additional groups of prisoners. This dramatically changed the character of the camp, the structure of the prisoner society and, above all, the prisoners' living conditions. When the Bergen-Belsen concentration camp was liberated on 15 April 1945, British soldiers found thousands of unburied bodies and tens of thousands of severely ill prisoners.

It is estimated that 52,000 prisoners from all over Europe were killed in the Bergen-Belsen concentration camp or died immediately after its liberation as a result of their imprisonment.

After effects of war

I look in the mirror and what do I see,

The face of a soldier, staring back at me.

I might look the same, I can still see and hear,

But what people don't realise, is that I'm hiding my fears.

The shadows round my eyes, hide the death and destruction I've seen,

The horrors I've been through, at night haunt my dreams.

I can't tell my family, they wouldn't understand,

The voices in my head, play like a brass band.

The images of war, invade my sleep,

Go round in my head, like a record on repeat.

The old me is long gone, he left when war came,

And the man who came back, just isn't the same.

I'll keep these feelings hidden, I'll try and get on with my life,

Do my best for my children and my devoted wife.

I'll never speak of what happened but the war will take its toll,

For though it may be over, it'll always be imprinted on my soul.

The Poppy

The poppy is a flower, like no other one,
It grows on barren land, where battles were lost and won.

Growing in places, where other flowers can't grow,
Where once were battlefields, now graves lie row by row.

A beautiful flower, it stands out amongst the leaves,
It's bright red petals, blow gently on the breeze.

A symbol of respect, for all those who didn't survive,
For those who gave their futures, so we could be alive.

And that's why we should wear our poppy,
with honour and with pride,

To give thanks for and remember, all those
who served and died.

BRITONS
"WANTS
YOU"
JOIN YOUR COUNTRY'S ARMY!
GOD SAVE THE KING

Conscripted

I'm just a lad of eighteen, never been away from home before,
But now I've been conscripted, I've got to go to war.

My friends are excited but it just fills me with dread,
I don't want to be one of those, who are maimed or left for dead.

I don't want to leave my parents, for I'm their only son,
I don't want to kill people, I've never even fired a gun.

I don't want to be coward, yet I don't want to fight,
I don't know what to do, I don't know what's right.

But I know if I stay, life wouldn't be the same,

I'd be handed white feathers, my family
wouldn't cope with the shame.

So off to war I'll go, in my uniform I'll stand
proud and tall,

Off to do my duty, I'll give it my all.

On the beaches of Dunkirk

We're stranded on the beaches, waiting for help to come,
Trying to evade capture, or being killed by German guns.

There's hundreds of thousands of us waiting, tired now of the fight,
We've been here for days, does anyone know of our plight?

German planes fly overhead, dropping bombs and firing bullets,
We have no way of taking cover, our only protection is our helmets.

Tired, cold and hungry, some men are so weak they can barely stand,
Whilst others lie injured, on makeshift stretchers on the sand.

And then one day on the horizon, a spectacular sight we see,
Hundreds of boats of all sizes, all together on the sea.

From war ships to rowing boats, they're all coming our way,
A cheer goes up, they're coming to save the day.

For some though it's too late, they paid the ultimate price,
On the beaches of Dunkirk, they made their sacrifice.

Christmas Truce

It'll be over by Christmas, that's what everyone said,

But the fighting continues, so many are already dead.

Looks like we'll be spending Christmas, here in the trench,

Amongst all the mud and bloodshed, the dirt and the stench.

The war's taken its toll, we're old before our time,

Young men we were but now past our prime.

Christmas Eve evening, a sound reaches our ears,

Of the Germans singing carols, a delight to hear.

Messages were shouted across, the trenches now full of laughter and smiles,

Christmas cheer spirit, spreads for many miles.

The very next day, the Germans appear on No Man's Land,

Today we are friends they say, we've come to shake your hand.

We climbed out of our trench, stood facing one another,

For today we weren't enemies but just like each other.

A slap on the back, a shake of the hand and then we were friends,

It might be just for today but none of us want the camaraderie to end.

I speak to this lad Hans, he tells me about his family and I tell him about mine,

He's barely eighteen and the only son out of nine.

He wants to be home, he didn't want to come here and fight,
Until now he'd never fired a gun, he didn't think killing was right.

Like me he was conscripted, we're really just the same,
Neither wanted to fight, we're just a pawn in a game.

We swapped photos, talked and laughed like old friends,
Shared cigarettes and food, both wishing this day wouldn't end.

But then the time came, when we had to say goodnight,
For tomorrow was a new day, we had to resume the fight.

Hans looked sad, as I bade him farewell,
Remember me my friend, if I don't survive this living hell.

The very next day at first light, the fighting began,

Bullets were flying, from man to man.

Sometime later, as we cross No Man's Land,

I came across a body, one I recognised by the ring on his hand.

A wave of sadness swept over me, for the young lad that only yesterday I met,

But Hans don't you worry, I will never forget.

We may have been on different sides and usually fighting one another,

But I'll always remember Christmas Day, when we were just like brothers.

In Mourning

Mothers and fathers, in mourning for their sons,

Brothers and sisters in mourning, for siblings with whom they once had such fun.

Children in mourning for beloved fathers, or the ones they never got to know,

Girlfriends and fiancées lose lovers and wives become widows.

Factories lose workers, colleagues lose friends,

When is this war, ever going to end?

Houses are bombed, people lose their homes,

Families torn apart and some people left all alone.

This war affects all of us, the Germans don't care,

But the people of Britain, a fighting spirit they share.

Remembrance Day

Remembrance Day, a time to honour the
brave,
To reflect on their lives and the sacrifice they
gave.

Some had no choice, they were conscripted to
fight,
Whilst others volunteered, doing what they
thought was right.

Some were leaving home, for the very first
time,
To go off to battle, to be cut down in their
prime.

Some were newly married, others had a child
on the way,
But all were united, when war came that day.

Marching off they went, little knowing what was in store,
Nor knowing how many, would not return from the war.

Fighting in the trenches, where so many paid the price,
Fighting for a future, so future generations could have a better life.

Each year in November, we remember with pride,
A generation lost, for us they died.

Remembering the young boys, women and men,
Who laid down their lives, never to be seen again.

We lay wreaths at memorials and poppies on
graves,
On Remembrance Day, we honour the brave.

IN
REMEMBRANCE

The Evacuee

I heard Mum and Dad talking, I've got to be
evacuated I heard them say,
I don't know what it means but sounds like
I'll have to go away

I don't see why I have to leave my friends and
family, why do I have to go?
But it seems I have no choice, Mum and Dad
say it's for the best and they should know.

And then the day dawns, Mum and Dad walk
me with my suitcase to school,
They've come to see me off and give me a set
of rules.

Be good they say and do what the people say,
Write and let us know how you are, maybe
we'll get to visit one day.

I climb aboard the coach, my parents wave me goodbye,
I wave back as the coach departs, whilst trying not to cry.

We have to then get on a train, I've not been on one before,
It's taking us to the country, we don't know what will be in store.

How long will we have to stay, will we ever see our parents again?
It all seems uncertain, life just won't be the same.

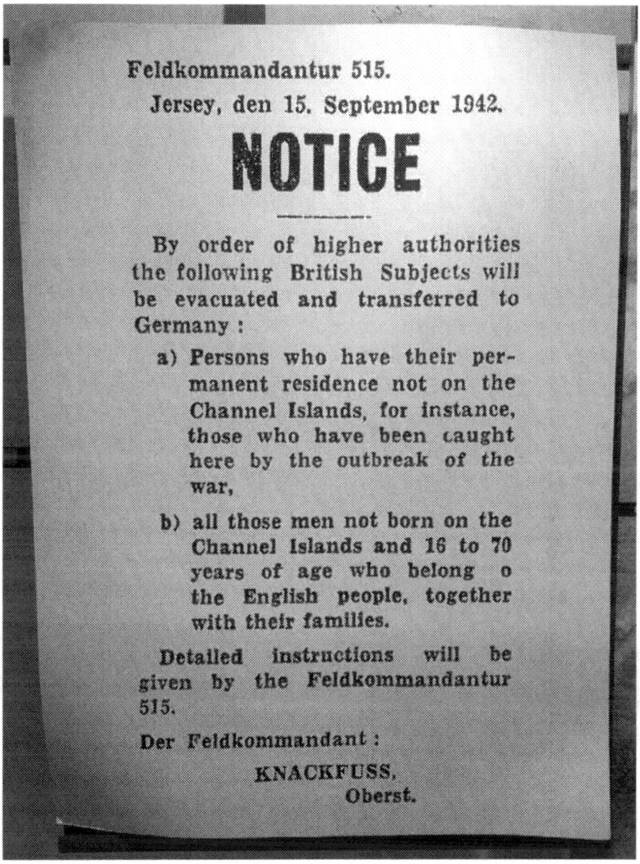

Feldkommandantur 515.

Jersey, den 15. September 1942.

NOTICE

By order of higher authorities the following British Subjects will be evacuated and transferred to Germany :

a) Persons who have their permanent residence not on the Channel Islands, for instance, those who have been caught here by the outbreak of the war,

b) all those men not born on the Channel Islands and 16 to 70 years of age who belong o the English people, together with their families.

Detailed instructions will be given by the Feldkommandantur 515.

Der Feldkommandant :

KNACKFUSS,
Oberst.

Prisoner of war

In memory of Edwin Gregory and Albert Edward Prior

One minutes we were in the trenches, the next we've been captured by the Hun,
Forced to walk for miles, at our backs are German guns.

Shouting at us in a language, none of understand,
Loaded onto lorries, off to a camp in a foreign land.

The journey seems to take hours, it's getting dark by the time we arrive,
The camp looks foreboding, will we make it out of here alive?

There's hundreds if not thousands of people here, all looking thin and weak,
And their voice is just a whisper, when they try to speak.
The regime here is strict and as the weeks go by,
Illness is rife, many of my comrades succumb and die.

The weeks turn into months, like those before us, we're now all skin and bone,
And all that keeps us going, are thoughts of home.

Each day is a struggle, we do our best to survive,
How long will this war last, will we make it out of here alive?

White Feather

I was walking home from work today, like I
do every day,
When a woman crossed the road and started
coming my way.

I thought nothing of it but then out of the
blue,
She stopped right in front of me and spat on
my shoe.

She spat at me again, other people started to
stare,
I asked her what the problem was, all she did
was glare.

She called me a coward and said that I should
be ashamed,
That I was doing nothing, when so many were
being killed or maimed.

A crowd had gathered, some of whom I
recognised you see,
But they joined in or kept silent, none of them
stood up for me.

Some of them started shouting and calling me
horrible names,
And the woman pressed a white feather in my
hand, I felt such shame.

Little do they realise, I tried my best to enlist,
Even when they rejected me, I continued to
persist.

I did everything I could, even about my age I lied,
I wanted to fight, to honour my brother and cousin who had died.

They rejected me on health grounds, due to a problem I had a child,
Despite passing the other criteria, from the list they had compiled.

The crowd were still jeering, even those who had known me for years,
I turned and walked away, I wasn't going to let them see my tears.

I hid out at a friend's house, whilst I waited for the crowd to go,
If only they knew, the heartbreak my family knows.

Later I catch a bus to a different city and sign up under a different name,
I just about pass the medical, I can now hold my head up high and not feel ashamed.

I can now walk down the streets and when people look at me,
They won't see a coward but a soldier they will see.

Sometime later when I'm home on leave, I see the woman who gave me the white feather that day,
I cross the road towards her, 'do you remember me?' I say.

Conscientious Objector

In memory of Stephen Hobhouse

War has come to our country, many have joined up to fight,
My brother is one of them but I don't believe killing is right.

I know some people see it as their duty, whilst others see it as fun and are doing it for the thrill,
But taking a life isn't the answer, I don't see why we should have to kill.

People call me a coward and place white feathers in my hand,
But my conscience is clear, on my values I know where I stand.

So many are against me and make me out to
be in the wrong,
But making a stand against something takes
courage, I've got to remain strong.

The authorities are trying to make me serve
but on my beliefs, I'll not quail,
I have to go to a tribunal but eventually end
up imprisoned in jail.

Blood Red Tears

The sky it cries, blood red tears,
For the many lives lost, throughout the years.

Of men, women and boys, who came to fight,
Who died in action, day and night.

Amongst the battlefield, now they lie,
Buried where, they fell and died.

The landscape looks after them, they can now
stand at ease,
Ghost of soldiers, now rest in peace.

For those who gave their lives, for us today,
They did us proud, in every way.

May 5th, 1943.

BREAD RATIONING

As from Monday, May 10th, 1943, the Bread Ration for the Civil Population is, until further notice, fixed as follows :

Manual Worker, male, over 21 years of age .. .. 4 lb. 12 oz.

Manual Worker, female, over 21 years of age .. 4 lb. 4 oz.

Other Adults, over 21 years of age .. .. 3 lb. 12 oz.

The Bread Rations of the rest of the civil population remain unchanged.

E. P. LE MASURIER,
President,
Department of Essential Commodities.

Zur Veröffentlichung genehmigt
Jersey, 5. Mai 1943.

Für den Feldkommandanten

DR. CASPER,
O.K.V.R.

VE Day 75

Seventy-five years ago, an end to the war in
Europe finally came,
But for so many families, life wouldn't be the
same.

For during the six long years of war they'd
lost friends and loved ones, in the fight
against the Hun,
So many young men and women, whose lives
were over before they'd even begun.

Six long years of rationing and blackouts,
evacuation and bombings too,
It was a time of hardship but a fighting spirit
saw them through.

Never did people imagine, that peace would
finally be here,
It was a day of celebration, a time for laughter,
fun and cheer.

A time to think of their loved ones who were
fighting, they could return home at last,
A time to look to the future, the war could
finally be a thing of the past.

A stiff upper lip and fighting spirit, through
the war years had helped people cope,
But now there was peace in Europe, people
could finally have hope.

We should think of those who returned
injured, who were never quite the same,
As well as the men, women and children left
at home, for it wasn't just those fighting,
whose lives were changed.

And now all these years later as we celebrate the anniversary, we should think of those who never made it home,
Who sacrificed their lives and are forever gone.

When you see a poppy think of me

At this time of year, many poppies you will see,
I hope when you see one, you'll think of someone like me.

For I was a soldier, for my king and country I did my best,
Killed in action on the battlefields, where I now finally lie at rest.

Before I went to war, I'd never left the country or fired a gun,
But off I went to fight, for a better future for generations yet to come.

I left behind the life I had and the future I could make,
When I said my last goodbyes, my family's hearts did break.

Fighting in the trenches, wishing it was home we could go,
Instead we're in foreign lands, fighting against the foe.

I don't think future generations realise, the sacrifices people like me made,
The true cost of war, the price our families paid.

We gave up everything, our tomorrows never came,
And now just a grave or memorial, commemorates our name.

The poppy is a sign of respect, to all those
who serve and to those who died,
And that's why at this time of year, it should
be worn with pride.

And when you wear your poppy, remember
the men and women like me, who were so
brave,
For we are the lost generation, who for you,
our lives, we gave.

Will you remember me?

I've got to go away my dear, I wish I didn't
have to go,
They say it is our duty, we've got to fight the
foe.
Will you remember me?

I've got to go across the sea, across to foreign
lands,
To fight in the trenches, with a gun placed in
my hands.
Will you remember me?

It's time for me to go my love, I've got to say
goodbye,
Be brave for me my darling and try not to cry.
Will you remember me?

I'm writing this from the trenches, it's cold,
muddy and damp out here,
Every day I think of you and wish that you
were near.
Will you remember me?

If I shouldn't make it, if on the battlefields I
should die,
Please don't mourn forever, please don't sit
and cry.
Will you remember me?

One more thing before I go my dear, I'm
sending all my love to you,
I hope whatever happens, my love will
always see you through.
I hope you'll always remember me

Dunkirk 80

Eighty years this year, since troops were stranded at Dunkirk on the beach,
Hoping against hope, that help was within reach.

There was nowhere to take cover, when the German planes were taking fire,
For days they were waiting, the situation seemed dire.

But then one day on the horizon, hundreds of boats appeared,
At last there was hope, that help was finally near.

Boats of all sizes came to the rescue, to help them all, they tried,
But despite their best efforts, so many men still died.

On the anniversary, we think of those who
survived and had a chance,
And remember those who died, whose lives
were lost on the beaches of France.

My Young Lad

My young lad is leaving, he's going off to war,
I'm very worried about him, for I've seen it all before.

I saw it in the last war, when my generation went off to fight,
They were young men like my lad is, whose futures were so bright.

For some of those who went, they never returned again,
Whilst those that did return, were never quite the same.

It was meant to be the war, to end all other wars,
I didn't think we'd ever have to, face it all once more.

My young lad is leaving, full of enthusiasm and fun,
But he's never been away from home before, he's never held or fired a gun.

I worry for my boy, I wish he didn't have to fight,
The situation concerns me and keeps me awake at night.

Off to war my boy goes, with bravery and courage he'll face the Hun,
And I know that whatever happens, I'll be proud to call him my son.

Battle of Britain 80

They were known as The Few, the fighters in the skies,
Never knowing each mission, whether they'd live or die.

Many not even out of their teens, young men they were, without a care,
Prepared to do their duty, ready to do battle in the air.

Full of enthusiasm, so many of them newly trained,
The life span of a crew was short, they knew they could be killed or maimed.

Taking on the Luftwaffe, they put up a great fight,
Taking part in bombing raids, during the day and at night.

For those whose planes went down, many now lie beneath the waves,
Commemorated on memorials, they have a watery grave.

Facing death on each mission, with bravery and courage they flew,
Their names went down in history, they're remembered as The Few.

Now on the eightieth anniversary, we remember those brave fighters of the skies,
They took on one last mission, forever they'll fly high.

Shot At Dawn

In memory of the 306 soldiers who were shot at dawn during WW1.

Underage I was, when I first joined up to fight,
To go and do what I thought was my duty, fighting day and night.

Two years have passed now, I'm still a lad, barely eighteen,
But I won't ever forget, the horrors of war I've seen.

I've fought in many battles, risking life and limb,
Each time thinking, the chances of making it out alive are slim.

I may only be eighteen but this war is making me feel old,
My nerves are constantly on edge, on my mind and body it's taking a toll.

The voices and noises are so loud, as they whirl around my head,
And when I try to sleep, all I see are images of the dead.

My hands shake and tremble, I can barely hold a gun,
But I've been passed fit for duty, I've got to still face the Hun.

We've been given new orders, we've got to go over the top,
But when the time comes, I'm frozen on the spot.

The gunfire is deafening, I cower in the trench in fear,
I try to block it out, running down my cheeks are tears.

I don't know how long I sit there but all goes quiet and my comrades come back at last,
And what happens next, seems to happen so fast.

For next thing I know I've been court martialled, for cowardice they say,
But until today I'm no coward, I've risked my life each day.

I don't know what happened, today just seemed so tough,
It all got too much for me, I'd finally had enough.

I tell them that I'm ill, if I was a coward I
wouldn't have signed up underage,
My fellow comrades try and support me but it
just puts the commander in a rage.

No one believes me, a doctor is sent along,
He passes me as fit and the trial doesn't last
very long.

I have no representation, they find me guilty
and sentence me to be shot,
I write a letter to my parents, telling them I'm
in a tight spot.

I worry for my parents and family, there's a
stigma to being shot for cowardice you see,
I'll become just a bad memory hidden away,
no one will speak again of me.

I'm choosing not to be blindfolded, so I can
look them in the eye,
Facing them with courage, until the time I die.

With fellow comrades amongst the firing
squad, with bravery I face my execution date,
Shot at dawn I was, my pardon came too late.

Dear Reader

If you have enjoyed reading this book, then please leave a review on Amazon.

Thank you.

Printed in Poland
by Amazon Fulfillment
Poland Sp. z o.o., Wrocław

55415225R00060